Stark County District Library
www.StarkLibrary.org
330.452.0665

JUL   2013

D1317595

Exploring Earth and Space

Exploring Earth's Surface

Ronald Granger

PowerKiDS press™

NEW YORK

Published in 2013 by The Rosen Publishing Group, Inc.
29 East 21st Street, New York, NY 10010

Copyright © 2013 by The Rosen Publishing Group, Inc.

All rights reserved. No part of this book may be reproduced in any form without permission
in writing from the publisher, except by a reviewer.

Book Design: Katelyn Londino

Photo Credits: Cover Cedric Weber/Shutterstock.com; p. 4 (mountains) Aibolit/Shutterstock.com; p. 4 (plains) Pakhnyushcha/Shutterstock.com; pp. 4, 16 (glacier) meunierd/Shutterstock.com; p. 4 (canyon) ozoptimist/Shutterstock.com; p. 5 Gallo Images/the Agency Collection/Getty Images; p. 6 Catmando/Shutterstock.com; p. 7 rob3000/Shutterstock.com; pp. 8, 15 Stockbyte/Thinkstock.com; p. 9 Digital Vision/Thinkstock.com; p. 10 Image Source/Thinkstock.com; pp. 11, 20 (rocky shore), 22 iStockphoto/Thinkstock.com; p. 12 © iStockphoto.com/codyphotography; p. 13 Todd Klassy/Shutterstock.com; pp. 14 (small waterfall), 21 Ablestock.com/Thinkstock.com; p. 14 (large waterfall) Ritu Manoj Jethani/Shutterstock.com; p. 17 Natapong Ratanavijittakorn/Shutterstock.com; p. 18 Galyna Andrushko/Shutterstock.com; p. 19 kojihirano/Shutterstock.com; p. 20 (beach) Zoonar/Thinkstock.com.

Library of Congress Cataloging-in-Publication Data

Granger, Ronald.
Exploring Earth's surface / Ronald Granger.
    p. cm. — (Exploring Earth and space)
Includes index.
ISBN 978-1-4488-8839-9 (pbk.)
ISBN 978-1-4488-8840-5 (6-pack)
ISBN 978-1-4488-8570-1 (library binding)
1. Landforms—Juvenile literature. 2. Earth—Crust—Juvenile literature. 3. Earth—Surface—Juvenile literature. I. Title.
GB404.G73 2013
551—dc23
                             2012011544

Manufactured in the United States of America

CPSIA Compliance Information: Batch #WS12RC: For further information contact Rosen Publishing, New York, New York at 1-800-237-9932.

Word Count: 394

Contents

Looking for Landforms

It's fun to **explore** Earth's **surface**. You can see many different kinds of land when you're exploring. These are called landforms.

A Look at Volcanoes

Earth has many **layers**. The top layer is called the crust. Under the crust, it's very hot. It's so hot that rocks **melt**!

The melted rock comes out of the earth through volcanoes. A volcano is a tall landform with a hole on top. After the melted rock comes out, it cools to form new land.

How Volcanoes Work

Melted rock comes out of the earth through a volcano.

Melted rock cools to form new land.

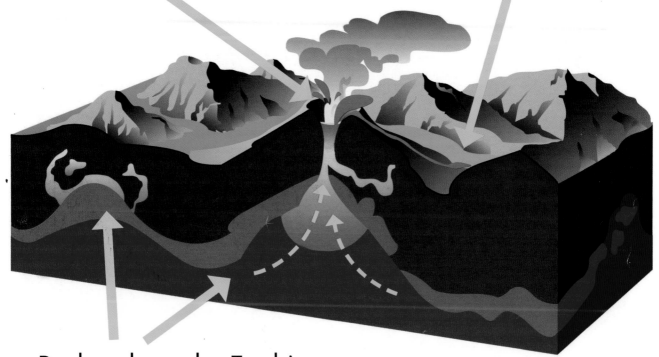

Rock melts under Earth's crust.

Tall Landforms

Earth's crust is made of pieces that are always moving! They move very slowly. Mountains are made when pieces of the crust push against each other.

Mountains are very tall landforms. They rise much higher than the land around them. The tallest part of a mountain is its peak.

A plateau (pla-TOH) is a tall landform, too. It's different from a mountain because it doesn't have a peak. It has a flat top.

Life on the Plains

Plains are also flat landforms. Plains aren't high like plateaus. They're low landforms.

The Great Plains are in the United States. Many kinds of grasses grow there. Many animals make their homes on the Great Plains.

Plains are good for farming. There are many farms on the Great Plains. We use the wheat that farmers grow there to make bread.

Waterfalls

A waterfall is another kind of landform. It's a river that goes over a **cliff**. Some waterfalls are small, and some are very big!

Visiting Valleys

Some rivers run through valleys. Valleys are low landforms. You can find them between mountains.

Some valleys are made by glaciers. A glacier is a huge piece of ice. Glaciers grow bigger as more snow falls on them.

Glaciers start to move when they get too heavy.

A moving glacier can cut through the ground.

This makes a valley.

A canyon is a special kind of valley. You can find a canyon between two cliffs. Canyons are very deep landforms.

Rivers run through canyons. In Arizona, you can see the Colorado River running through the Grand Canyon.

On the Coast

A coast is a kind of landform that many people visit.
It's the land along a sea. Some coasts are sandy.
Some are rocky.

The land on a coast is always changing! The water from the sea changes the way a coast looks.

Time to Explore!

There are many landforms on Earth to see and learn about! What kinds of landforms would you like to explore?

Glossary

cliff (KLIHF) A high, steep piece of rock.

explore (ihk-SPLOHR) To search something to find out more about it.

layer (LAY-uhr) A piece that goes over or under another piece.

melt (MEHLT) To change from hard to soft using heat.

surface (SUHR-fuhs) The top part that can be seen.

Index

canyon(s), 18, 19

cliff(s), 14, 18

coast(s), 20, 21

Colorado River, 19

crust, 5, 7, 8

glacier(s), 16, 17

Grand Canyon, 19

Great Plains, 12, 13

layer(s), 5

melted rock, 6, 7

mountain(s), 8, 9, 10, 15

peak, 9, 10

plains, 11, 13

plateau(s), 10, 11

river(s), 14, 15, 19

valley(s), 15, 16, 17, 18

volcano(es), 6, 7

waterfall(s), 14

Due to the changing nature of Internet links, The Rosen Publishing Group, Inc., has developed an online list of websites related to the subject of this book. This site is updated regularly. Please use this link to access the list: www.powerkidslinks.com/ees/surf

3 1333 04173 9622